FIND YOUR WAY HOME

6 TRUTHS ABOUT GOD, JESUS, AND CHRISTIANITY

BRANDON C. REGO

Find Your Way Home: 6 Truths About God,
Jesus, and Christianity

Copyright © 2017 by Brandon C. Rego

Published by Sojourn Publishing, LLC.
ISBN: 978-1-944878-44-3

TESTIMONIALS

What a refreshing read! The thoughts of Brandon Rego come from a serious mind and pure heart. His desire is to correct cultural misconceptions about Christianity's core truths, so that people might discover that God is better than you were told!

Rev. Dr. William A. Lewis, Senior Pastor

Brandon Rego has taken his Christian walk and placed it into a compelling journey through the truth of the Bible. This young author, with a heart like that similar to David's (after God's) has articulated a message about what it means to ask the hard questions about faith and and by trying to answer them he is teaching others on how they can find their way to Christ. Well done.

Mary Downey, Director of Missions,
Community Presbyterian Church
Executive Director, Community Hope Center.

Brandon Rego is the new generation of leaders in the ministry. In his book, "Find Your Way Home: 6 Truths About God, Jesus, and Christianity," he debunks common myths of Christianity. As a next generation leader, Brandon represents the "now generation." His insights and enthusiasm about God and his walk with God is refreshing and also inspiring. Brandon is well on his way to becoming a renowned ministerial leader, author, and teacher. As a scholar-practitioner and ministerial leader, I strongly recommend you read Find Your Way Home: 6 Truths About God, Jesus, and Christianity. It's a delightful read.

Dellroy O. Birch, Ph.D.;
Executive Pastor, Experience Church

Brandon Rego's heart for Jesus and for sharing the liberating power of the Gospel is evident in *Find Your Way Home*. This book is a great reminder that true reconciliation with God cannot be achieved through good works or our best humanly efforts. Instead, eternal salvation is only provided through God's grace in the redeeming blood of His son Jesus Christ, and Jesus' work on the cross.

Norm Caldwell; South Florida,
Lifework Leadership Coach

If truth sets you free then believing a lie about yourself or about God will keep you arrested. In *Find Your Way Home*, Brandon invites you to capture the ideologies that keep you chained down and allow God's truth to be fully recognized in your life. It's this kind of counterintuitive wisdom that wrecks our egos and re-ignites a genuine relationship with our Creator. Whether you're trying to figure out if Jesus is who he said he was or you're an accomplished pastor with professional designations all around your name, this book will invite you into a level of self-discovery and introspection that may just refine your thoughts about God's place in your life altogether. Thank you Brandon for not telling the world what the world wants to hear but speaking the truth that it so desperately needs. I'm so very proud of the man of God you've become. Keep writing. The world is reading.

Jeremy D. Young; Youth Pastor/Teacher

This is an exceptionally important book which should be read, re-read, and inwardly digested by all Christians, anyone wanting to learn more about God, and anyone seeking truth in general.

Lloyd Regas; Streamcare Corporation

An insightful and emotional interpretation of what you thought you already knew. It will deepen your faith.

Adam Parrish; Disney

Brandon is such an amazing writer for his 22 young years and based on his bio, he has already accomplished more than some do in a lifetime. *Find Your Way Home* is a fantastically readable , positive story with truths for all ages. I'm sure that it was intended to try to reconnect the younger set and Millenials who have given up on God, Christianity, and religion or never wanted it in the first place, but when I picked up this manuscript, it was very hard to put down because it brings forward such profound truths in such a clear, simple expression of faith and logic that it is important for all generations everywhere. Sometimes people are confused by the Bible with all its historical stories, parables, and the words of Jesus as put down by the disciples. After all, it was written over more than a thousand years by many different authors even though inspired by God. Yet, it remains applicable to our lives today as it has to people over the last several thousand years. As Brandon points out, it has over 800,000 words and can be daunting, even to some who have read it several times. People can get lost and not find their way home to God, Jesus, and Christianity. Brandon brings out some of the greatest messages and truths in the Bible in such a clear and understandable way that it will give those who read it a way to reconnect and "come home" to a life of love and everlasting life. This inspiring manuscript will encourage many I hope to take another look at Christ and Christianity from the perspective, as Brandon puts it, of the greatest love story ever written—the Bible. I'm sure you will find Brandon's book, as I did, uplifting and compelling. As an elder for the Community Presbyterian Church in Celebration, I pray that Brandon continues to provide powerful, positive expositions of our faith as he has in *Find Your Way Home.* Enjoy his inspirational work and pass it on to bring the family of Christ together and to our home in Him.

Dr. Bruce A. Carlson
Elder of Community Presbyterian Church in Celebration
Owner Imagination Realty, Inc.
Retired VP Operations for Dupont Performance Coatings
Former CEO of Blue Sky Solar , LLC

This book by Brandon Rego is thoughtful, insightful, and readable. This read was thought provoking and well-written. I would recommend this book. Good Stuff!

Pastor Dorrell Briscoe has a Masters of Theology from Liberty University and is currently working on his PhD in Ministry at Duke University.

CONTENTS

INTRODUCTION

One truth I've come to understand in my life is that the Bible is, without a doubt, the longest love letter ever written by anyone to anyone. God had a lot to say about our relationship with Him and the unfathomable lengths He went to restore it. His words have moved across time, space, and history to guide us back into perfect harmony with Him, and that story isn't even over yet. Though we do know that, in the end, God is successful in bringing His people back into that harmony.

This love letter to mankind, the most-read book in history, is actually not a book. It is a collection of sixty-six books, scrolls, texts, and letters made up of more than 800,000 words. Obviously, God had a lot to say!

Of course, every Christian, and every *person,* is fallible. I certainly am. Even with a work of such totality as the Bible, sometimes we have a tendency to put words in God's mouth. I know I have.

We don't do it on purpose (usually). Most of the time it's not literally misattributing quotations to God that He never said. It's more about certain beliefs, ideas, and images we hold in our minds about the nature of God and how this thing called "Christianity" is supposed to work. Many of the things we imagine are not even our own ideas, but thoughts that have been passed down culturally for thousands of years.

When I was a child, I used to imagine heaven as being situated on white puffy clouds in the sky. You probably did too. Now you (probably) and I both know that's not really what heaven is supposed to look like. But where did that even come from? Is it an idea we all came up with as children, by coincidence? No, not at all. This idea is way older than any of us. 1 Thessalonians 4:17 mentions Christians being "caught up in the clouds to meet the Lord in the air." Some people take that literally and some don't, but either way, that's not a description of heaven.

It's a cultural idea, not a biblical one, that heaven is in the sky and the clouds. This is reflected in all sorts of artwork from almost any era in human history, whether a medieval painting or a modern Internet comic strip. This is what I mean when I say that we put words in God's mouth. He never said that this is what heaven looked like. Actually, He said something very different.

But this is just a silly example, and pretty harmless.

I was raised Christian, but I didn't choose it for myself until I was about eleven years old. Since then, as any other Christian will tell you, it's been a daily learning experience and one that never ends. Slow as I was to learn, my ideas about God are very different from what they were back then. One of the most important parts of that learning process was to shed ideas that were cultural, not biblical. This is important, because a lot of these ideas are damaging to hold in anyone's personal relationship with their Creator and Savior. And these ideas grip a lot of people. Me too, sometimes. I have to remind myself that a lot of these things aren't true, because my brain defaults to them. Of course it does, because most of us are raised with these ideas.

Why does it matter? Jesus once told a story (Luke 15:11-32) about a lost boy. The young man told his father he wanted his inheritance early. He received his wish and left. He went out into the world, where he spent and gambled away all the money he was given. By the end of it, he was so ragged and destitute that the only work he could get was feeding pigs. And even then, he was so hungry that the pig food started to look good.

In the end, the young man returns home to beg his father's forgiveness and ask for work, but his father runs to him and embraces him, overjoyed at the return of his son.

What snapped the young man out of it and made him realize he needed to go home? He had become so accustomed to filth that pig's food seemed appetizing. Perhaps he remembered that he once lived in a mansion and realized that he could do so much better than pig food if he returned.

That's us! Certainly I've experienced it. Pig slop is what the world has to offer, as far as spiritual food. They're the ideas that our cultures offer us about God and Christianity: half-truths or outright lies. But when we spend so much time around it, sometimes it starts to seem like good food. Especially if we've never known better. That's why we need to either remember our Home or learn about it. Because when you turn to head home, your Father will run to meet you on the road, embrace you, and feed you love and truth. Home is where you find real spiritual nourishment.

You may be reading this introduction wondering if this book is for you. It probably is, whether you're a Christian or not. If you are a Christian, you will look at these myths that I and others have believed, and my hope is that it will save you some time in moving past them for yourself. If you're not a Christian, you probably have an interest in God or you wouldn't be reading a book like this. My hope for *you* is that if I expose some of these myths, it might give you a better vantage point from which to look at Christianity. And of course save you time if you do become a Christian.

Lastly, my goal here is not to soften the Bible and make it more palatable for people, nor is it to try and whip people into shape and make them think God is "gonna' getcha" if you don't get some more hard-boiled ideas about the Bible.

I'm just a regular guy. I'm neither a theologian, nor an expert. All I intend to do is to present some lessons *I've* learned personally and back them up with the Scriptures from which I learned the lessons. It is my prayer that you find this useful in some way, and that it may save you some time in walking your own path with the Lord.

Now, let's take a look at some things God never said...

(A note to Bible scholars:

I will be using the New Revised Standard Version [NRSV] for most of my quotations from the Bible. A couple of times I will use the New Living Translation [NLT] or New Life Version [NLV] for understandability. Nearly every quote will denote which version I am using. If I do not denote the version, it is from the New Revised Standard Version)

CHAPTER 1

Pig slop: *"God sends people to hell to be
tortured for all eternity."*

Food from Home: *"For I have no pleasure in the death of
anyone, says the Lord God. Turn, then, and live."*

EZEKIEL 18:32 NRSV

Yup. Hell. The big one. There's probably not a single more objected-to idea in Christian theology and not a single more misunderstood concept than Hell. It's probably the thing that's caused the most internal anguish amongst Christians, and the most disdain amongst atheists. All my life, I've never known anybody who actually likes the concept of Hell (except in rare moments of extreme anger toward people who commit heinous crimes).

But here's the thing: God doesn't really like the idea either. All the internal pain and anguish that people go through thinking about Hell is mostly founded on an unbiblical myth about what Hell is, and that's why I want to start here.

What do you envision when you think of hell? Quick. First instinct.

I don't have to be a mind reader to guess that you probably envisioned some dark place filled with burning fire and tormented people. Maybe a burning lake where people are in constant pain, as punishment for "not believing."

Even if you've been a Christian long enough to know this isn't exactly accurate it's still probably the first thing you imagined. I want us to try and leave this imagery behind us. Why? Because when we imagine things as worse than they are, it damages our perception of God. That's neither fair to Him, nor good for us! Also, this particular image we hold, like the much less harmful image of heaven we talked about before, is mostly a result of art and culture rather than the Bible.

"But wait," maybe you say, "I specifically remember the Bible describing it this way!"

Technically correct. But there's more to the picture in this case.

Jesus makes reference to Hell many times in the New Testament. It's described as a place of darkness, a place of eternal flame, and a place of wailing and gnashing of teeth. More specifically, it is described as a "lake of fire" in the Book of Revelation, which is where that particular piece of imagery comes from.

But here's the thing. A basic reading of the New Testament reveals that Jesus liked *very* much to speak in stories and parables. When Jesus gave a lesson, it was rarely as simple as just making His point directly. I used to wonder why He would complicate things instead of just speaking plainly (not that He never did, just not all the time). But, with time, I came to realize that Jesus used parables and stories for two reasons.

First, He used stories full of imagery because human beings relate to stories much more than we do to simple lessons. Anyone who doubts just how much we love our stories need only look at the size of the storytelling industries. Books, movies, television and web series; the list goes on and on. Storytelling has been *the* human pastime and favorite hobby for as long as our history. Naturally, Jesus knew this too, so most of the time His points were made in the form of a story.

Plus, stories are more easily remembered and internalized than lessons or sermons.

Secondly, Jesus usually preferred to make His points through stories because it would force people to actually think about the point He was trying to get across. How many times in our lives have parents or teachers tried to make a point to us, but it went in one ear and out the other? People tend to like minor puzzles almost as much as they like stories. So Jesus would tell a parable, and His audience would be forced to think about the meaning of what He said. This way, once they figured it out, they definitely wouldn't forget it. The only time Jesus explained what His parables meant was *after* people had spent some time trying to figure it out.

A tertiary point is that Jesus *loved* to say shocking things. Think about it. What's one of the most oft-repeated sayings of Jesus?

"Turn the other cheek."

This comes, of course, from Jesus's most famous lesson, the Sermon on the Mount. He wanted to make a point that His followers should not seek revenge. He could have done this in two ways:

He could have said, "Don't seek revenge."

Or He could have chosen to say something very shocking and exaggerative to get the point across in a way that people would remember. So He said:

"But I say to you, Do not resist an evildoer. But if any-
one strikes you on the right cheek, turn the other also;
and if anyone wants to sue you and take your coat, give
your cloak as well."

MATTHEW 5:39-40 (NRSV)

That statement – "Turn the other cheek." – is still in our vocabulary two thousand years later.

7

Now, was He actually telling people never to physically defend themselves? Of course not! Later on He tells His disciples to buy a sword for the road just to be safe, so the message definitely wasn't "don't defend yourself." Jesus's goal when He taught us to "turn the other cheek" was about an attitude, a way of treating enemies and people who wrong us, accidentally or intentionally. And that is to not seek revenge.

If we understand that this was Jesus's teaching style, then why do we assume His sayings about Hell must be literal?

Let's go back to the "lake of fire" in Revelation.

Now, Revelation is a very, very complex book and difficult to wrap one's mind around. But what is *not* hard to understand about Revelation is that it is completely *dripping* in symbolism and allegory. Even if we don't know completely what those symbols and allegories mean (Or, I should say, I don't. Some believe they do know what it all means), we know that they're not to be taken literally.

At least, they *shouldn't* be taken literally. When we take allegorical or poetic writing literally, we cheapen its worth and destroy its usefulness. While some believe taking every line of the Bible literally is being faithful, it's actually much more faithful to examine and ponder the true meaning of what is said. If we don't, we miss a lot. Sometimes, we miss everything.

For example, when the book of Revelation describes Jesus descending from the clouds with a sword in His mouth, are we to understand that in the Second Coming of Christ, Jesus will literally arrive with a sword clamped between His teeth? Of course not! That's completely silly to take at face value.

Yet, Christians often don't apply this logic to the "lake of fire." Fire, which, in the Bible has long and often been used as a *symbol* of judgement, not a literal judgement. There are no two ways around it, because Revelation even qualifies this outright when describing the lake.

> *"Then Death and Hades were thrown into the lake of*
> *fire. This is the second death, the lake of fire."*

REVELATION 20:14 (NLT)

Why does the imagery linger and often get interpreted so literally, then? Once again the answer is usually art and culture. I was once browsing the Christian section at my local bookstore, and a book caught my eye about a man who claimed to have been sent to Hell by God so he could return and tell people what it was like. His depiction was horrifying. Worse than anything ever described in the Bible. He spoke about unending torture so terrible that it took him some thousands of years to realize that the ambient sound was his own screaming.

What a terrible and untrue depiction! And yet this is what a lot of people envision. Ultimately, I guarantee you he made a fair bit of money selling that book. As we just learned, to say shocking things in art or storytelling *sells*.

Whether it was ancient Greek depictions of Hades, or *Dante's Inferno*, or such modern books about Hell, human society likes to use these images in our art. And we teach each other that art represents reality. It's especially easy to do for such a taboo subject.

At this point you may be thinking, "Well, gee, that's all well and good, but if the *symbolism* of Hell is that bad, what's the reality? What happens when God sends someone to Hell?"

Well, there's a whole lot that we don't know about Hell. But there are at least a few things that we do know.

The first and most important thing about Hell is that it's not a place that God sends people. It is a place we must choose for ourselves. Hell isn't the place where some bitter toddler-god tosses people for not worshipping him. The truth is, there is nothing more emotionally painful for God than when people choose Hell.

We saw at the beginning of this chapter that God takes no pleasure in any of this. When God says He takes no pleasure in something, He means *none*. Zero. Zip. Not the slightest hint. Not the stray thought of pleasure that the worst human being ever to live should enter Hell. God takes *no* pleasure in it. And if that's the case, then what's left for Him to get out of it?

Pain.

Please let this sink in, because it's so important to grasp this when we try to examine the character of God.

Who do you love most in the world? A parent? A sibling? A child? A friend? Imagine that person going up to you and telling you that they don't want anything to do with you ever again, as long as either of you live. And they're dead serious and they won't change their mind.

How do you respond to that? Force yourself on them and *make* them have you in their life? Probably not. Do you get angry? Furious? Maybe. But above all, the thing you and I would feel in a moment like that is a profound sadness. Possibly depression. Definitely an emptiness. Even if we got angry, when that faded we'd be left with just the pain. But most of us would let the loved one go, because they have the right to go and we don't have the right to stop them even if we're certain it's in their best interests.

This is what it's like with God, people, and Hell. Hell is a place specifically designed for people who go through their entire lives, ignoring every call on their hearts, every plea from God to allow Him into their hearts and lives. Hell is for people who decided that they didn't want God in their lives.

So, what does God do with that decision? He loves us more than anything, so, naturally, He lets us go.

Only one problem: Where can we possibly go to get away from God even if we want to? It shouldn't be possible. So, God creates the one place in the entirety of existence where He will *not* be. A special place just for people who want to be away from Him. That's Hell. And that's all Hell is. Nothing more, nothing less. A place created for the specific purpose of honoring the human desire to be away from God. It's not a torture chamber. It's just a place set aside.

To the Christian, a place where God is totally absent can sound like the worst possible thing. For us, it would be. And I definitely don't want that for you, dear reader. But the Christian's priorities are different from the rest of the world. It's hard for us to understand that some people don't want God.

Am I suggesting that a certain kind of person might *prefer* Hell to Heaven?

I don't know. Depends on the person, I suppose. Especially if it's understood not to be a torture chamber. It's a question I cannot answer with any certainty, but I can't shake the feeling that it's a possibility for some.

On the other hand, you might now be wondering, after what I've said, if Hell is actually a punishment at all? Is it actually "bad" for the person who chooses it? Is it fair that everyone should receive the same treatment? And what about people who never heard of God?

Well, first, yes, it is a punishment. But not as you might think. I will elaborate in a moment.

Second, the Bible says that not everyone will have the same experience in Hell. For one example of proof, there is a moment when Jesus discusses towns that would, in the future, drive the disciples away.

> *"Truly I tell you, it will be more tolerable for the land of Sodom and Gomorrah on the day of judgment than for that town."*
>
> MATTHEW 10:15

The takeaway from this passage is that not everyone will have the same experience.

God is not unfair and would not classify someone like Hitler or Stalin with Joe the atheist. And although it's little explained, God *promised* that people who never heard of Him will also be treated fairly.

So, is Hell actually bad, considering all we've learned? Yes, it is. Of course it is! Heaven is unimaginably superior to Hell in every possible way. That's why Hell is described as a place of wailing and "gnashing of teeth." Though those aren't symbols of eternal physical torture, they *are* symbols of eternal, ultimate regret. The wages of sin is death, and spiritual death (the second death).

Hell won't be a good place, objectively speaking. But *subjectively*, anyone can convince themselves of anything, including the idea that they are and will be happier without God in their lives. The punishment is that the people in Hell should, by actually receiving what they wanted, miss out on something so indescribably better.

Just because God knows what's best does *not* mean that He will force that on us if we choose otherwise. He respects our free will and He loves us too much not to allow us to make our own decisions. In those ways, Hell is a gift to the people who choose to reject God.

Still, comparing Hell to Heaven is comparing pig slop to fine gourmet cooking. Heaven, which was bought for you with the life of Jesus, is the far greater gift. I'm convinced that only misinformation or outright self-deception could cause someone to reject this gift. I really hope that's not you, but if it is, keep reading. Whatever ideas you have about God, I guarantee you, He's better than what you imagine.

CHAPTER 2

Pig slop: *"God helps those who help themselves."*

Food from Home: *"It is the Lord who goes before you. He will be with you; he will not fail you or forsake you. Do not fear or be dismayed."*

DEUTERONOMY 31:8 NRSV

Of all the things in this book, learning the truth about this false saying of God was perhaps the most surprising on some level. There are many ideas we keep that we know something is wrong with, but I thought this was actually a true line from the Bible itself. I was *taught* it was true as a child by a friend, and I heard it many other times growing up.

But, as usual, it turns out that God is better than this. By a long shot.

First, this line *never* appears in the Bible, anywhere. Once again, this is a concept borrowed from antiquity. The idea that supernatural powers only act on behalf of those who are already solving their own problems is found in some of Aesop's fables. "God helps those who help themselves" comes from an English politician named Algernon Sydney, who lived in the 1600s.

Actually, Algernon Sydney's philosophies and political theories are widely considered the foundation of modern Western values, especially the values that ultimately led to the founding of the United States of America. The values we hold at the core of American culture are the ones first espoused in English politics by Sydney (and a contemporary, John Locke), which explains why this myth is so prevalent in the United States. The quote is still spoken by some politicians and pundits in our modern politics.

Sydney had a lot of revolutionary ideas about freedom, self-determination, and the rights of the people to change corrupt forms of government, but he could not have been more wrong on this one thought about God.

There are two problems with the saying, both very damaging to the individual's relationship with God and society as a whole.

The first problem is rooted in why people say this at all. Whether it's a politician on TV or a regular person in regular conversation, I've only ever heard this phrase used as a reason *not* to help someone who needs help. Maybe your experience with it has been different, but I'm willing to bet it's similar.

Personally, I've only ever heard it used in reference to the most desperate and needy members of society, which makes me both angry and sad, because there's nobody God reaches out to more than the outcasts of society. To say the opposite? That's practically slander.

I've heard it said of the homeless; I've heard it said of those in recovery programs (and why those programs should be eliminated); I've heard it said of people who lost their jobs and homes in the economic crash of 2008; I've even heard it said to me about myself.

Many Christian Americans take pride in their country being a "Christian Nation." Some people agree with that idea and some people don't, but one thing is certain: The central theme of the Bible is *not* self-sufficiency. The central theme of the Bible is that humanity needed help to be in a relationship with Him, and God in His grace and love provided that help. That's key.

Christianity is the only religion in which a person's fate is not based on what the person does. It's not about being good enough or improving or being worthy of God or heaven or anything like that. Christianity is unique in that it is the only religion where God reaches down to lift man out of the pit rather than telling man to climb out of it. That's what makes it amazing!

This puts Christianity in sharp contrast to the traditional "I'll do it myself" culture of the U.S., so maybe it's not surprising that this saying is so often attributed to the Bible. There's absolutely nothing wrong with going out and accomplishing awesome things. But this false saying of God cannot be used as an excuse not to help people who need help. After God lifts us out of the pit, our task is to act as His hands and feet. That means a Christian's job is to share God's love in the way He freely offers it to anyone who needs help.

Remember who we are supposed to mimic. We don't get to decide who's "worthy" of help and who needs to "help themselves." Grace, by definition, is unmerited. If God had extended love only to those who were worthy, nobody would receive it. Instead, He offers it to all. We are meant to do the same.

There is one other problem with this saying, just as harmful as the first.

The beauty and trouble with ideas is that they burrow into our minds and become invisible parts of our identity and way of thinking. Most of us don't know the ideas that form our personalities and beliefs. And those who do only know a few.

When this particular idea takes hold in a person's mind, it can create a lot of grief. When someone believes that God helps only those who help themselves, it means that whenever they have a hard time in life, whenever God "feels" distant, whenever things are going badly, that person will believe that God has turned His back on them because they're not doing enough.

This is incredibly damaging to the relationship between us and God. And nothing could be further from the truth, anyway. Although God doesn't promise an easy-breezy life for His people, He does promise that He will never leave us or forsake us. He promises to be a solid foundation, like rock, that we can build our lives on. He promises that no matter how bad things get, He will create some good out of the situation. He promises that He will never let us go, and that we can hold on to Him as an anchor. And, finally, He promises that every pain will be washed away and overshadowed by glory in the end.

God helps anyone who comes to Him for help. Always.

CHAPTER 3

Pig slop: *"Make a deal with God."*

Food from Home: *"Look at the birds of the air; they neither sow nor reap nor gather into barns, and yet your heavenly Father feeds them. Are you not of more value than they?"*

MATTHEW 6:26 (NRSV)

Bargaining. Most of human civilization is based on bargaining and trading and buying and selling. Everything we do revolves around deal-making. It's completely ingrained into our consciousness, so much so that we even think of things like *war* in terms of bargaining. ("Paying the price in blood.")

Even *gift-giving* is about bargaining for a lot of people. I know I'm guilty of this one. When I receive a gift from someone, I feel obligated to give that person a gift of equal or greater value. Or worse, I remember giving someone a gift of certain value, receiving one back of lesser value, and feeling a bit salty about it!

If, in theory, I were not the only person who has done that, and it was a thing that happened often in our culture, it would further prove that everything (in our minds, anyway) is about bargaining.

Have you ever tried to give someone a gift, and then you had to convince them that they didn't owe you anything in return? Happens all the time.

So much so that even God Himself experiences it. All the time, as a matter of fact. More than anyone.

Because bargaining, buying, and selling are such cornerstones of our ways of life, we apply this to God as well. It can be difficult to accept the idea that He doesn't want anything from us in return for what He promises us. After all, He promises so much, and it cost Him so much. Surely we have to do something in return?

Let me address one thing up front. Whether or not we "owe" God anything is a separate question. Obviously, as God gave us life, and then gave us eternity, we owe Him everything. But this is a matter of love and devotion, and we will talk about it later on. The thing to understand here is that God's promises are not based on a transaction in which we have to buy His gifts or His provision with our deeds.

Plenty of times, especially when I was younger, I've gone to God in prayer with whatever concerns and requests I've had on my mind. And I'd promise to do things if He would only fulfill these requests. I think we all have done that!

But as I got older, my thinking shifted. I fell into a trap that I want you to avoid at all costs.

I knew in my head that God didn't work on a bargaining basis. So I wouldn't pray like I was making a trade or writing a contract. Instead, it just became a lingering doubt that followed me. The idea that if I didn't do enough good or if I made too many mistakes, God would withdraw His care because I had not upheld my end of the "deal."

I felt, and still occasionally feel, that if I do good, good things will come to me, and if I do bad, bad things will come to me.

This idea is called "karma" and it is the basis of every religion in the world, *except* Christianity (Christianity flies in the face of karma). Our bargain-based society is obsessed with karma, though. We are preoccupied with Justice and Fairness. You commit a crime? You "pay" your "debt" to society, by fine, or by jail time. Sometimes even death is the price.

Is it wrong that someone should be punished for a crime? No, of course not. That's how the world works, that's even how God works. Karma is a fair system. You get in return what you put out. You put out pain? You get pain. You put out love? You get love.

Except for one thing. God wasn't satisfied with karma being the sole basis of His relationship with His beloved Creation. Karma is logical, fair, and even just. But it's also cold. Thing is, God isn't a God of cold logic alone. He's a God of burning emotion! He loves us far too much to let karma and justice and bargaining be the dictators of our relationship with Him.

But, a good king does not flout his own laws, either. So, God intervened and took our karma onto Himself. And that is called Grace.

Grace, which is unearned favor, is the basis of the Christian faith. *This* is what sets Christianity apart from all other religions. This is what makes Christianity amazing! Other religions say we must reach out to God via the laws of karma. Christianity says God reaches out to *us* by His grace. It is so utterly different from what the world usually teaches about God.

Grace is not about us and what we do. It's about God and what He does. And what He does is offer that grace, freely, dispelling karma out of our spiritual lives, where He wants it to have no hold.

This is real spiritual food. I want you to take it into yourself and let it push out all the garbage you've had in the past. If you do, you'll be opening up an eternal relationship with the living God, and that's priceless.

Now, that doesn't mean we'll always have what we want. But it does mean we'll always have what we need. That's what

Jesus was saying in the verse at the start of this chapter. That verse comes from a passage about worry, wherein Jesus tells us not to worry, because there is no benefit, nor any need.

When you're a Christian, you don't need to worry about holding up "your end of the deal." Because there was no deal. All there is, all there ever was, was love. And whatever we *do* from that point on is a response to the love that is constantly poured onto us.

If you want proof that you didn't and don't have to earn anything, that it was never about a "deal" and never will be, put your hand on your chest.

Feel your heartbeat. With every beat, it sends the power of life coursing through you. By that power, every one of the thirty-seven trillion cells in your body receives all it requires to live, and by that power, all that needs to go is removed. Now, you tell me, what did you have to do to earn it?

You know the answer to that question. Every single beat of your heart is the free gift of God. If He didn't still want you here, it wouldn't keep beating. And for the Christian, this gift of life goes beyond even the very last beat of our heart.

So don't be afraid. Your relationship with your Creator, or your Savior, is not contractual. It's not a deal, or a bargain. There is no buying or selling or karma or anything like that involved. When you need something, go to God boldly and ask. You'll be shocked at how ready God is to pour blessings on your life if you're willing to receive. But more importantly, even when things go badly, and even when *we* go badly, He will always be there. That's His promise. No costs. No bargaining. No strings attached.

CHAPTER 4

Pig slop: *"Don't ever question God."*

Food from Home: *"If any of you is lacking in wisdom, ask God, who gives to all generously and ungrudgingly, and it will be given you. But ask in faith, never doubting, for the one who doubts is like a wave of the sea, driven and tossed by the wind,"*

JAMES 1:5-6 (NRSV)

This mythical statement of God in particular is not necessarily as common as the others. In fact, it's more common among non-Christians than Christians, in my experience. Many non-Christians are repulsed by the idea of a God that requires a completely blind trust with nothing to go on. Obviously if a normal person, a stranger, asked for absolute trust without question, you'd probably tell them to take a hike!

But there are also Christians who believe this idea that God demands we not question Him. They're doing themselves no favors. The sad truth is, they're putting a limit on the depth of their relationship with God.

How can this be the case? Well, in Luke 10:27, Jesus teaches us that the most important commandment is "You shall love the Lord your God with all your heart, and all your soul, and all your strength, and all your mind." Generally, people who say "God is not to be questioned" mean well. They're trying to love God with all their heart, soul, and strength.

But that is incomplete. God doesn't want you to make yourself blind and mute to follow Him! He doesn't just want your affections. He wants your *mind* as well. This is another thing that sets Christianity apart from other religions. Many religions teach that God cannot be understood. Christianity elevates the mind's love to be equally important as the love of the heart, soul, and our own personal grit.

How does the Mind love? It engages, it studies, it thinks, and it learns. And that is all through the power of questioning. A question is the most powerful tool of the mind, and the greatest means by which the mind can grow. The mind is a gift to be used, not cast aside.

There are a lot of confusing things in the world. Why do things happen? Why does God let them happen? When pain comes, it is no sin to beat on the chest of God and say, "Why?" Dozens of Psalms are dedicated to this, and they were written by King David, who was described as a man after God's own heart. And if that weren't enough, the entire Book of Lamentations is dedicated to this.

If *even* that weren't proof enough, then consider that Jesus Christ Himself, God's own son who has known the Father for all eternity, cried out to Him in this way:

> *"And about three o'clock Jesus cried with a loud voice,*
> *'Eli, Eli, lema sabachthani?' That is, 'My God, my*
> *God, why have you forsaken me?"*
>
> MATTHEW 27:46 (NRSV)

Questioning is not off limits.

So, what do we do when something happens in our lives, or we can't understand some aspect of God or His word? The answer is in the verse at the beginning of this chapter. We pray, *confidently*, for wisdom and understanding. And the promise is that if we pray with that confidence, we will receive wisdom, without exception.

But what about that caveat? The second part of the verse, says the person who asks for wisdom but does not believe is like a wave in the sea being tossed around. What does that mean?

Well, it means two things. First, if you ask without really expecting anything from it, you're not really asking, are you? So you remain like a cork in the ocean, floating around with no anchor. You won't get anything if you don't expect to get it when you ask. That applies in life and that applies to God. Why? Because even if you receive, you won't recognize it because you already decided you wouldn't receive.

The second meaning is just as important. There is a *kind* of questioning God does not appreciate in the slightest. And that is when we impugn His character. The proof of God's good character is clear, given that He sacrificed Himself to save our lives. Not to mention giving us life in the first place. Doubting His character is insulting to Him. As it would be insulting to any human being. If a firefighter dies saving someone from a blaze, we wouldn't dream of doubting that firefighter's character.

You can question God. You can even question Him on the really hard stuff, like Habakkuk, who said,

> *"Why do you make me see wrongdoing and look at trouble? Destruction and violence are before me; strife and contention arise."*
>
> *Habakkuk 1:3 NRSV*

You can even rant. Like David.
> *"Why, O Lord, do you stand far off?*
> *Why do you hide yourself in times of trouble?"*
>
> PSALM 10:1 NRSV

It's all about the intention of your heart. Habakkuk and David, even if they were exasperated, questioned God with sincerity, not in an accusatory way. Ultimately, they still trusted God. You can see this pattern in many of the pain-filled Psalms. David may start the poem with questioning, but by the end he makes it clear he still *trusts* God and His character.

As for Habakkuk, he got his answer. God responded by saying,

> *"Look at the nations, and see! Be astonished! Be astounded! For a work is being done in your days that you would not believe if you were told."*

HABAKKUK 1:5 NRSV

Then God shows Habakkuk a vision of what was coming to liberate the Jewish people (the Babylonians, who would throw down the Assyrians). Whenever someone in the Bible questioned God with sincerity and humility, they got their answers. Those answers were reaffirmation that God has a plan in motion for ultimate good.

Habakkuk ends his book with a prayer, stating that even when things look bad, he knows he can lean on God and trust Him.

This is the way it is for all of us. In times of doubt or times of pain, don't think God doesn't want your questions. Take your questions to God. Do what James 1:5-6 says. Approach God and ask for His wisdom and His understanding. Do it with honesty, expect to receive, and you'll find that your questioning of God leads to greater trust, not less. It opens up a whole new dimension to your relationship with your Creator.

Ask away.

CHAPTER 5

Pig slop: *"You're perfect just the way you are."*

Food from Home: *"It doesn't matter whether we have been circumcised or not. What counts is whether we have been transformed into a new creation."*

GALATIANS 6:15 (NLT)

I can hear the howls of anger all the way from here, where I sit writing these lines. So give me a moment and I'll explain why this particular false saying of God is actually *good* to let go of, and not at all contradictory to anything we've learned so far.

Here, we have a mythical belief that prevails usually among more liberal Christians (whereas, some of the other beliefs may have stronger footholds among conservative Christians and churches).

Among all the great Bible-based churches in the world, I believe there are basically three types of "problem churches":

The first are the prosperity churches that care only about extracting every dollar from their congregations.

The second are the churches that are so conservative that they create an unloving and un-Christian atmosphere that cares far more about "rules" than loving God and loving its neighbors.

The third are the Christian churches that are so liberal in their beliefs that they essentially invite people to "come as you are...and stay that way." This is the kind of Christian and/or church that I'm talking about with this false saying.

Often when we teach each other that we're perfect as we are, it comes from a loving place and it isn't the same as believing it in the context of being perfect and complete, in and of ourselves. At that point, it becomes a corruption of a truth that actually keeps you down, more than anything.

In Psalm 139:14, King David says,

"I praise you, for I am fearfully and wonderfully made; Wonderful are your works; that I know very well."

Every human being (including *you)* was "fearfully and wonderfully made" in the very image of God. There's no questioning that you were made to be perfect. Yet we live in a corrupted world. Nothing of this Earth is perfect anymore. But there's still hope!

I have many friends who follow New Age philosophies, and they share this perfection myth a lot. We all struggle (I know I do) to look inside ourselves and stare our flaws in the face. It's hard to admit we're not perfect, but if we're honest, it's an obvious reality. And only when we admit that we're flawed can we have a real relationship with God.

Here is the *real* truth that gets twisted, and you can take this to heart: "You may not be perfect, but God adores you anyway, and if you make Him your God, He will continually make you New." We become perfect and complete only when we allow God to fill us with His Spirit.

If we convince ourselves of *our own* perfection, and go to God with that state of mind, what are we even doing? What's the point? To say "I'm perfect, in and of myself" is just a way of saying "I don't need God." It's dishonest in every possible way. If I do that, I'm lying to myself, lying to God, and lying to everyone else. And no real relationship is founded on lies. Only by recognizing that perfection comes from Christ's spirit living in us can we truly be perfect.

We are, all of us, in need of our Creator's hands to mold us. And He will. That's a promise.

> *"I am confident of this, that the one who began a good work among you will bring it to completion by the day of Jesus Christ."*
>
> PHILIPPIANS 1:6 (NRSV)

However, there is something more. This myth comes in another "flavor," so to speak. Sometimes, someone will go to God with the idea that they need only say a prayer, get "saved," and carry on with their lives as normal.

"Wait," you might say. "Haven't you been saying for most of this book that Christian salvation is not based on what we *do*?"

Yes, I have been saying that. And it's true! But the Bible teaches us that Faith without Works is dead. The point is that if we truly have made Jesus the Lord of our lives, and we have truly allowed His spirit to take residence within us, we will actually care about what He wants. It's the difference between doing good in order to work our way into heaven, and doing good as a response to the God who *gave* heaven to us. The reaction to such a gift should be to at least *try* to do good. If we believe we're perfect in inaction, we may not realize the importance of acting on our faith.

Using Abraham as an example, the Bible says this:

> *"You see that faith was active along with his works, and faith was brought to completion by the works."*
>
> JAMES 2:22 NRSV

What actions are these? Personally, I don't think it's complex. I believe God approves of anything you do that makes you *grow* in your faith and knowledge of Him, and anything you do that *contributes* to your fellow man in His name. Especially when we share His Gospel with others as part of it.

When we do this, we have the opportunity to walk with God in a way that will make us grow into more than most people even dream. If we pray and listen for His promptings, our lives can truly be extraordinary.

CHAPTER 6

Pig slop: *"You've gone too far this time."*

Food from Home: *"My little children, I am writing these things to you so that you may not sin. But if anyone does sin, we have an advocate with the Father, Jesus Christ the righteous."*

1 JOHN 2:1 (NRSV)

In this verse we meet Jesus Christ, Attorney at Law.

Just kidding, of course. But there is actually some truth to that.

Here, once again, we have a myth that fools a person into thinking that some aspect of their relationship with God is determined by what *they* do.

Are you seeing a theme with these false ideas we sometimes believe about God? When it comes right down to it, most of these myths have the same root. Think about that for a moment, and we'll explore that root in the last chapter, after we examine this final myth that has given me a lot of headaches.

When I was a young Christian, I believed this whole-heartedly. I thought that, while Jesus could and would wipe away all your mistakes once, after that, it was up to me to keep clean. Maybe I thought that I could go back and get "re-wiped" whenever I made a mistake. And again, and again, and again. But, ultimately, it was my responsibility to "stay good." And I know I'm not the only one because I've met a lot of people who go through this. Especially newer Christians.

But that's not really how any of this works. Humans just couldn't ever be "good enough" to earn their own way into heaven, because the standard for Heaven is a 100% spotless record. Completely out of reach. That's why God had to come to the Earth and pay the debts of humanity with His own life. And He did it both from the perspective of a person giving their life for loved ones and that of a parent watching their child be tortured and executed...and letting that happen, for our sakes.

That's how much God cares about *you*, about *me*, and all of us. He was prepared to die for us without even the guarantee that we would allow Grace to cover us. God went through all that anguish just for the *chance* to spend eternity with you.

> *"But God proves his love for us in that*
> *while we still were sinners Christ died for us."*
>
> ROMANS 5:8 (NRSV)

As we all gradually grow into the perfection we have with God, we will make mistakes, as human beings. Everybody is at a different place as they walk their path. Some of us make more mistakes than others, but that doesn't mean that we're less Christian or not trying hard enough.

The lie that gets whispered when we make our mistakes is that we've erred one too many times, and God will no longer extend His grace to us.

If you're like me, you feel that while God may have been willing to forgive far worse from *other people*, when it comes to *you*, you've just gone too far too many times.

If you're like me, you have sometimes judged the health of your relationship with God by the way you *feel* about it. Does He "feel" close? Does He "feel" near?

We can't live like that. Remember this verse:

"The heart is devious above all else;
it is perverse—who can understand it?"

JEREMIAH 17:9 (NRSV)

That's not a condemnation of emotion, but this verse points out the truth that we can't live by what we feel. It's easy to allow our feelings about God push the actual truth out of our minds. God is always graceful, merciful, and present in your life if you've made Him your Lord. But we won't always feel that way, even though it's always true. That's why Jeremiah calls the heart "devious."

The verse at the beginning of this chapter says that Jesus Christ is the one who is truly righteous in this world. The only person who ever lived the perfect life. He alone is in the position to condemn, having been through all the trials, temptations, and pains of our human lives, and coming through those without so much as one moment of failing. He could condemn us, if He wanted to.

But He never did. Instead He chose to suffer and die at human hands, for our sakes. And even after all that, He now stands by the Father's side, choosing to be our *advocate*. He speaks to the Father on our behalf. And if the only one who can condemn us chooses instead to advocate for us, who's left to condemn us? Ourselves? Actually, no. If we're in Christ, even we aren't capable of condemning ourselves, only making ourselves "feel" condemned in our hearts.

So when we miss the mark (which is the meaning of the word "sin"), we can either believe the lies that will bubble up in our minds, or we can use the moment as evidence of why we need to lean on God's grace, and try to do better in the future.

I'm not saying that God doesn't *care* when we sin. He has no intention of letting anyone use Him as a "get out of jail free" card. And if someone is trying to use His grace as a license to do whatever they want, then He's not really their God, is He? And that's what really counts. So we should always try to be more like Jesus. We will fail, but in trying, we prove our faith (and we'll make it a lot closer to the mark trying to reach it than not trying to reach it).

If God truly is *our* God, and we've made Jesus our Lord, and we care about His opinions, and we're relying on His grace, then we have it. That's the promise. We can't "out-sin" God's grace for us.

> *"Sin spread when the Law was given. But where sin spread, God's loving-favor spread all the more."*
>
> ROMANS 5:20 (NLV)

If you've ever thought for a moment that you were powerful enough to outdo God's light with your personal darkness, well, I have news for you! You can't. None of us can. We're not nearly capable of it.

> *"...for my Father has given them to me, and he is more powerful than anyone else. No one can snatch them from the Father's hand."*
>
> JESUS CHRIST (JOHN 10:29 NLT)

Now do you really think that you can outdo that? Because that's what this chapter's lie teaches us. It convinces us that we have to *do* anything to keep our salvation. And by extension, that we *can* do anything. We can't. That's why we needed a savior in the first place. Do you think God would have gone through all that pain if we didn't need it? To push Him aside and try to work things out on our own by "being good," some would say, is an insult. One thing's for certain, it moves us away from God, not closer to Him.

Remember this the next time you start to think God might be finished with you:

God isn't bound by time like we are. I believe when Jesus Christ died on the cross and rose again, He took *all* our sins. Past, Present, and Future. The human being is not powerful enough to overcome God's love, which reaches through all of time and space to wash us clean, so we might spend an eternity with Him, and He with us, reconciled.

Put your hand on your chest again. Is your heart beating right now?

It is?

Well, then God still loves you, doesn't He?

CHAPTER 7

Now, in the previous chapter, I said that all six of these false statements have the same root. That's true. In fact, you could make a powerful argument that whenever anyone sins (again, "misses the mark") at all or gets a wrong idea about God, it comes down to the same root.

It's the same human problem, like a virus in our very DNA, that started every problem the world ever saw.

Pride.

Pride is the simple belief that we know better than God, or are more capable of directing our lives than He is. Pride is what drove the Prodigal son away from his home. It's something we all do from time to time. The less we do it, though, the better our lives are going to be. The less we do it, the closer we will be to God.

Every one of the false teachings we've talked about has its root in pride.

"God helps those who help themselves?"

"You've gone too far this time?"

"Let's make a deal?

To believe God would say anything remotely like those quotes requires us to believe that our actions determine how much God loves us. And when we think we determine God's actions, that's Pride. God's love is based on *Him*, not us. And He adores us not because of what we do or don't do, but because we're His children.

"Hell is a torture chamber?"

That quote goes hand in hand with the belief that God is so vengeful and vindictive that He created a special place just to make us regret our actions forever. And this is, once again, thinking that our actions determine God's actions. In reality, God combined justice with mercy and love, and also set aside a place for people who didn't want His gift of life.

"Don't question me?"

If we think God would say that, we think He could come to hate us for what we do wrong. Only this time, in asking questions, we wouldn't even be doing anything wrong! God doesn't want you to check your brain at the door. He wants your mind *too*.

"You're perfect just the way you are?"

No we're not. Not alone. If we think so, we're saying we don't need God. But we do, and *He* is what then makes us perfect.

In the end, this is what it all comes down to: I, and a lot of people, can tell you from experience that when you think you've got everything handled on your own, you're only kidding yourself. We, like the children we are, need the help of a loving parent to guide us. And we have a Father in heaven who wants to be with us. He'll take the Captain's wheel, but only if we stop trying to wrestle it away from Him.

The good news is that most Christians grow out of this! The bad news is that it usually takes some sort of severe problem or crisis to shock us out of the illusion that we know what we're doing.

So, whether *you* are a Christian or not, I'd like to invite you to let God take full control. Let Him guide your steps, because He knows what He's doing and we do not. When it comes down to it, if we choose to go Home, it's not us actually "finding" our way home. It's God guiding us back to where we belong.

Now, it's not easy to surrender like this, it's against our nature. I still fight myself on it all the time. But it *is* worth it, because when you know you have the Creator and sustainer of the entire Universe, in all its complexities, on your side, you can step out and do *anything* you're called to do with absolute certainty.

Can you imagine having that confidence? That passion? You can. The more you practice it, the more normal it becomes. And even when things don't go right, we know that they *will* be turned to good. And you'll often *see* it unfold.

At this moment, a lot of Christian authors would write some sort of prayer to recite in the hopes that you, if you aren't a Christian, will choose to repeat the words and become one. But I'm not going to do that. You can do that, but that's not what this is all about.

The great secret to living a God-led life is actually no great secret at all. There's no magic prayer. There's no ritual. This isn't religion, this is Christianity. It's a relationship with the Living God. All anyone needs to do is decide to have that relationship. Believe that Jesus was raised from the dead, decide that He will be *your* Lord and Savior, declare it to others, and live your life as your Heavenly Father's child. If you rely on His grace and love, not only will you get heaven, you'll gradually be changed from the inside out into a new creation. It's about what God has done for us, not what we can do for Him.

This is the Truth that Jesus said would set us free. Free from myths and lies that weigh us down, and make the waters murky. It won't be completely easy to live in the Truth, because the world (and our nature) will always try to pull us back to the old thoughts and the old ways. But if you choose to reject these false ideas whenever they enter your mind, and replace them with prayerful truth, they will lose their hold on you, and you will know true, unshakable peace.

I pray that you will always walk in the truth. And, if you're willing, I ask you do the same for me.

Be blessed.

"Grow in the loving-favor that Christ gives you. Learn to know our Lord Jesus Christ better. He is the One Who saves. May He have all the shining-greatness now and forever. Let it be so."

2 PETER 3:18 (NLV)

ABOUT THE AUTHOR

Brandon Rego is a 22-year-old Christian and author of both nonfiction and novels. Born and raised in Florida, he became a Christian at the age of 12 and began writing earlier than that. He always had a love of stories and believes that the right story could change a person for the rest of his or her life. At the age of 15, he decided to pursue writing as a career. He currently lives near Orlando, Florida where he is active in his church and the local community. He loves his family and friends and hopes to be of as much service as possible in this life.

www.ingramcontent.com/pod-product-compliance
Lightning Source LLC
Chambersburg PA
CBHW071747020426
42331CB00008B/2210